"Dear friend Mr. Adams. We love you very much. . . . We ask, we beg you to tell court let Mendi people be free."

—KIN-NA, IN A LETTER TO JOHN QUINCY ADAMS WRITTEN ON THE EVE OF THE *AMISTAD* TRIAL

THE *AMISTAD* MUTINY: FIGHTING FOR FREEDOM

BY BARBARA A. SOMERVILL

Content Adviser: Joanna Banks,
Museum Educator, Washington, D.C.

Published in the United States of America by The Child's World®
PO Box 326
Chanhassen, MN 55317-0326
800-599-READ
www.childsworld.com

The Child's World®: Mary Berendes, Publishing Director
Editorial Directions, Inc.: E. Russell Primm, Editorial Director; Emily J. Dolbear,
Line Editor; Katie Marsico, Assistant Editor; Matthew Messbarger, Editorial Assistant;
Susan Hindman, Copy Editor; Sarah E. De Capua, Proofreader; Marsha Bonnoit,
Peter Garnham, Terry Johnson, Chris Simms, and Stephan Carl Wender,
Fact Checkers; Tim Griffin/IndexServ, Indexer; Dawn Friedman,
Photo Researcher; Linda S. Koutris, Photo Selector

Cover photograph: Watercolor of the ship *Amistad* circa 1840, artist unknown /
© New Haven Colony Historical Society/AP/Wide World Photos

Interior photographs © New Haven Colony Historical Society/AP/Wide World Photos: 2;
Bob Child/AP/Wide World Photos: 30; Beinecke Rare Book and Manuscript Library, Yale University: 19
left and right; The Connecticut Historical Society Museum, Hartford (detail): 10; Bettmann/Corbis: 9, 21, 31;
Corbis: 18, 26, 35; Bowers Museum of Cultural Art/Corbis: 36; Hulton|Archive/Getty Images: 6, 20, 28;
AFP/Getty Images: 12; The Granger Collection, New York: 8, 11, 23; Library of Congress: 22, 27;
Library of Congress Manuscripts Division: 33; Naval Historical Center: 17; The New Haven
Colony Historical Society: 15; The Prudence Crandall Museum, State of Connecticut: 24, 25.

Library of Congress Cataloging-in-Publication Data
Somervill, Barbara A.
The Amistad mutiny : fighting for freedom / by Barbara A. Somervill.
p. cm. — (Journey to freedom)
Includes bibliographical references and index.
ISBN 1-59296-227-0 (lib. bdg. : alk. paper) 1. Slave insurrections—United States—Juvenile literature. 2.
Amistad (Schooner)—Juvenile literature. 3. Antislavery movements—United States—Juvenile literature. 4.
Slave trade—America—History—Juvenile literature. [1. Slave insurrections. 2. Amistad (Schooner) 3. Slave
trade. 4. Antislavery movements.] I. Title. II. Series.
E447.S66 2004
326'.0973'09034—dc22   2003027078

Contents

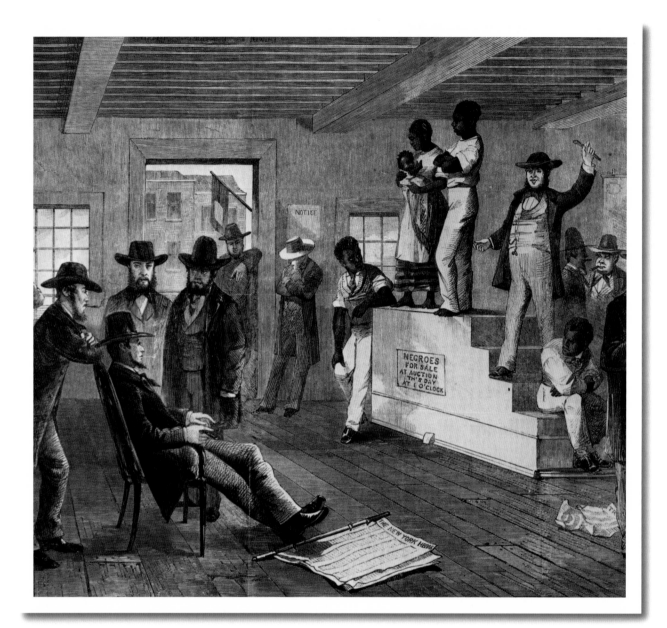

MILLIONS OF AFRICANS WERE SOLD AS SLAVES TO WHITE LANDOWNERS IN THE UNITED STATES.

The Sale of Human Beings

In 1492, Christopher Columbus landed on an island in the Caribbean Sea and claimed it for Spain. Other European explorers arrived after Columbus. They claimed land in the Americas for England, France, Portugal, and the Netherlands. European kings and queens gave away land in the Americas to friends and relatives.

The European landowners wanted to make money from their land. They built large farms, or plantations, to grow cotton, tobacco, sugar, coffee, and **indigo.** But many people were needed to work in the fields, and there were not enough settlers to do this job. The need for workers created a thriving business—the sale of human beings.

Estimates suggest that from the early 1500s to the late 1870s, more than 9 million slaves from Africa were shipped to the Americas. Millions died on the journey. The slave traders packed as many Africans in their ships' **holds** as possible. The captive Africans had to survive hunger, thirst, filth, and whippings. At slave markets, landowners inspected, bought, and sold Africans like furniture. After being bought, the enslaved people lived and worked in conditions that were often just as horrible.

In the early 1800s, **abolitionists** spoke out against slavery in the United States. Several northern states stopped traders from bringing new slaves to their shores. Some states banned slavery altogether. Yet, slavery continued to expand in the southern United States, as well as Brazil and Cuba. The slave traders, who were making a lot of money, kept shipping Africans to sell into slavery. The sale of human beings was a profitable business. The *Amistad* was one of the ships involved in this business.

The Dark Journey

The story of the *Amistad* begins in Africa. Sengbe Pieh was a farmer and Mendi tribal leader in a village in Sierra Leone. In April 1839, Sengbe Pieh was tending his crops when Africans from another tribe captured him. The men sold Sengbe Pieh to a slave factory on the Gallinas River.

The slave factory was a huge, open-air prison that housed hundreds of men, women, and children. They had no protection from the sun or rain. Most of the captives, in their 20s, were strong and healthy. They needed their strength to survive what awaited them.

CAPTIVES SUCH AS SENGBE PIEH WERE HELD IN SLAVE PENS ON THE GALLINAS RIVER IN SIERRA LEONE.

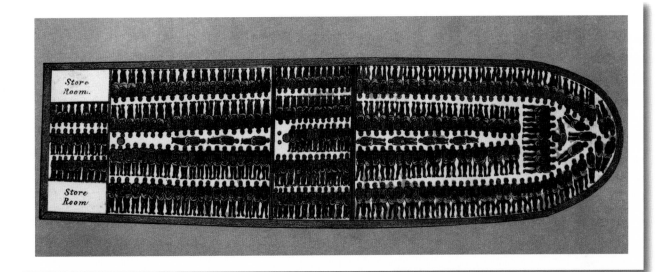

IN THIS DIAGRAM OF A SLAVE SHIP BOUND FOR AMERICA, HUNDREDS OF AFRICANS WERE PACKED INTO THE VESSEL'S HOLD.

That spring, the Portuguese ship *Tecora* anchored near the slave factory. The ship's captain bought more than 500 people, including Sengbe Pieh. The Africans were loaded aboard the *Tecora,* which was bound for Havana, Cuba. Crewmen stripped the Africans of their clothes and chained them together in twos. The slave traders stuffed the Africans onto shallow decks in the ship's hold. Barely 4 feet (1.2 meters) separated one rack of humans from the next. The traders packed the Africans like sardines in a can. The more slaves they delivered to Cuba, the more money they would make.

During the trip to Cuba, the Africans received very little water and some rice. Those who did not eat were beaten. Some ate until they vomited. Most of the time, the Africans lay on wooden racks, unable even to turn over. Because the hold had no bathrooms, they lay in their own body waste.

For two months, Sengbe Pieh and the other Africans suffered from seasickness, thirst, and hunger. Many Africans died on the trip. A slave trader usually lost about one-third of the ship's cargo—about 160 people. Those who survived arrived at the port filthy, thin, and sickly.

Finally, the *Tecora* anchored off Havana, Cuba, in June 1839. The slave traders unloaded their cargo late at night. Although bringing new slaves into Cuba was against Spanish law, the traders were able to get around the rules by calling the slaves ladinos, or people born into slavery in Cuba before 1820.

Then the slaves were cleaned, dressed, and fed. They had to look their best to fetch a top price. The slaves crowded into large prisons called **barracoons** until they were sold at the slave market.

Two Spaniards named Pedro Montes and José Ruiz bought slaves from the *Tecora*. Montes chose four children. Ruiz selected 49 adults, including Sengbe Pieh. He paid $450 for each slave. The two men also bought false papers stating their slaves were Cuban-born ladinos and changed the slaves' names. Sengbe Pieh was given the Spanish name Joseph Cinque.

On June 28, 1839, Montes and Ruiz loaded their 53 Mendi slaves onto a **schooner** called the *Amistad*. They worked in darkness to avoid Spanish inspectors. The word *amistad* means "friendship" in Spanish, but there was nothing friendly about life on this vessel. The ship's crew treated the slaves like animals. Male slaves had iron **shackles** around their ankles. Rough **manacles** cut their wrists. Metal collars linked one slave to another. The women and children were tied together with rope. Again, the Africans were forced below the main deck into a dark, airless hold. The *Amistad*'s hold was so shallow that the Africans sat crouched together, one behind the other. There was no room to stand.

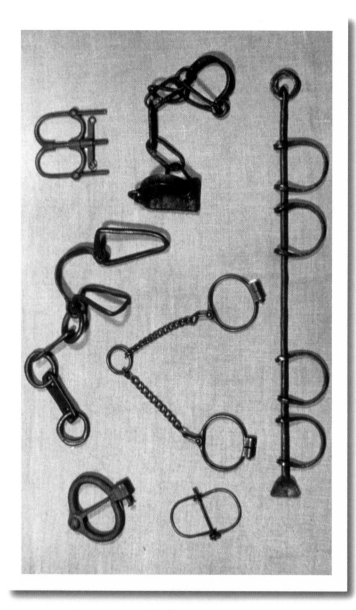

THE AFRICAN CAPTIVES ON SLAVE SHIPS WERE FORCED TO WEAR IRON SHACKLES AND MANACLES.

The captain of the *Amistad,* Ramón Ferrer, took pride in his speedy black schooner. Built in Baltimore, Maryland, the ship was sleek and easy to handle. Ferrer's crew included a black cabin boy named Antonio, a cook named Celestino, and two crewmen.

Ruiz and Montes owned the ship's extensive cargo. It included jewelry, dishes, silverware, cloth, other household goods, leather, gear for horses, and knives for cutting sugarcane.

A normal trip to the Cuban port of Guanaja took about three days. This time, storms struck the Caribbean Sea, and the *Amistad* drifted off course. The Africans, huddled in the hold, feared for their lives.

On the third day, Captain Ferrer realized the trip would take several more days. He cut the food and water rations for the slaves. A day's food for each slave was a banana, two potatoes, and a cup of water. When one of the Africans tried to take more water, a crewman whipped him.

Then, the *Amistad's* cook played a cruel joke on the slaves. Through hand signals, he told the Africans that the crew was going to kill and eat them. In the six months since his capture, Sengbe Pieh had seen his people jailed, starved, chained, and beaten. He had seen dead Africans tossed overboard like trash. Why would he not believe this frightening story? Sengbe Pieh talked with his fellow slaves, and they came up with a plan.

THE *AMISTAD,* SHOWN HERE AS A MODERN-DAY RECONSTRUCTION, WAS BUILT IN THE UNITED STATES. THE SWIFT SHIP HAD TWO MASTS AND A NARROW HULL.

Mutiny on the Amistad

On deck during mealtime, Sengbe Pieh found a loose nail and pried it free. Later that night, he used the nail to unlock his shackles. He freed his fellow slaves from their chains. The men searched the cargo for weapons and found the knives and some heavy sticks.

At around 4 A.M., on July 1, 1839, thick clouds covered the moon and stars. The slaves were ready. In the darkness, Sengbe Pieh and two other slaves named Grabeau and Burnah led the **mutiny**. The Africans poured onto the deck armed with knives and sticks.

The freed slaves slashed at the captain and his crew. Sengbe Pieh struck Captain Ferrer with his knife. Ferrer dropped to the deck, and other slaves strangled him.

Pedro Montes drew a knife and tried to drive the Africans back into the hold. The slaves did not retreat. They surged forward and hit Montes with knives, sticks, and oars. José Ruiz fought hard, but the Africans overpowered him, too.

In a short time, the Mendian slaves took charge of the ship. Captain Ferrer and the cook Celestino lay dead. The ship's two crewmen jumped overboard and probably drowned. The Africans lashed the cabin boy, Antonio, to the anchor but did not hurt him. Ruiz surrendered and begged that his life be spared. Montes suffered deep gashes during the short battle. He crept into the hold to hide behind some food barrels. When the freed slaves found him, Montes, too, begged Sengbe Pieh for his life.

AFRICAN-AMERICAN ARTIST HALE WOODRUFF PAINTED THIS MURAL OF THE *AMISTAD* MUTINY IN 1939. THE ARTWORK WAS COMMISSIONED BY TALLADEGA COLLEGE IN ALABAMA.

Sengbe Pieh and his fellow Africans now faced a serious problem. No one in the group knew anything about sailing a ship like the *Amistad*. They decided to spare Ruiz and Montes and ordered them to sail toward the rising sun in the East—toward Africa.

This plan seemed sensible since the *Tecora* had sailed toward the setting sun during their trip across the Atlantic Ocean. However, the Africans could not tell direction by the night sky. Ruiz and Montes used the slaves' lack of knowledge to trick them.

Ruiz and Montes sailed eastward during the day, as they were ordered. To slow the trip east, Montes allowed the sails to flap in the breeze. At night, however, the Spaniards let the sails fill with wind. They changed direction and headed northwest. They hoped to find another ship to save them.

The *Amistad* traveled a strange, zig-zagging course up the East Coast of the United States. Several ships spotted the *Amistad* on its odd journey. When the ships' captains saw armed Africans on the deck, they left the *Amistad* alone.

Food and water were in short supply. The original plan was to spend three or four days—not two months—at sea. The ship wandered along its course through July and into August. By this time, the Africans were faring poorly. Many became sick and died. Finding a port to buy supplies became urgent.

On August 25, 1839, the *Amistad* anchored off Culloden Point at the eastern end of Long Island in New York. Sengbe Pieh and several of the men rowed ashore to buy food, water, and supplies. They used Spanish gold to pay for whatever they wanted.

Near where the *Amistad* had anchored, the USS *Washington,* a survey ship, was mapping the shoreline. While on duty, Lieutenant Richard Meade spotted the Africans onshore. The ship's captain, Lieutenant Thomas R. Gedney, ordered Meade to investigate. The next day, Meade and a small crew boarded and took control of the *Amistad.*

Gedney estimated the slaves to be worth between $20,000 and $30,000, which was a small fortune then. (In 1839, the U.S. president's yearly salary was $25,000.) Gedney and his crew hoped to claim the *Amistad* and its cargo—including the slaves— as **salvage.**

IT WAS LIEUTENANT RICHARD MEADE, SHOWN HERE IN A PHOTOGRAPH FROM 1863, WHO FIRST NOTICED THE *AMISTAD* AFRICANS ON U.S. LAND.

Decisions and Disagreements

Now Lieutenant Thomas R. Gedney had to make a decision. Should he take the *Amistad* captives to a New York harbor or to Connecticut? Since New York had banned slavery, the *Amistad* Africans would not be considered property there. Connecticut still allowed slavery, however. There he could claim the ship and everything on it under salvage laws. With money in mind, Gedney ordered Meade to take the *Amistad* to New London, Connecticut.

After the *Amistad* and the USS *Washington* arrived in New London, Gedney sent a message to U.S. officials in New Haven, Connecticut. He and the USS *Washington*'s crew had claimed the *Amistad*, its goods, and the Africans as salvage.

THE USS *WASHINGTON* CREW TOOK THE *AMISTAD* TO NEW LONDON, CONNECTICUT. THIS 1854 ENGRAVING SHOWS THE BUSY HARBOR.

On August 29, 1839, Judge Andrew T. Judson held a hearing. He listened to Gedney's claims as well as Ruiz and Montes's story. Ruiz and Montes wanted the *Amistad* and all its cargo—including slaves—returned to them. Judson ruled that the Africans on the *Amistad* should be charged with mutiny and murder. Sengbe Pieh, the remaining 38 adult Africans, the cabin boy Antonio, and the four Mendian children landed in jail.

A bolitionists, led by New Yorker Lewis Tappan, quickly arrived to support the African prisoners. Because the Mendians spoke no English, they couldn't explain what had happened. The abolitionists looked for someone to translate English and Mendi. They eventually found a man named James Covey, who helped the Africans tell their side of the story.

There were several issues to be decided in the *Amistad* case. The first issue was where the case should be tried. Should the trial be held in New York or Connecticut and in federal or state court? The ship had been captured in New York waters, but it was brought to Connecticut for salvage. The second issue was who had rights in the case. Who could legally claim the *Amistad* and its goods? Several people claimed those rights: some New Yorkers who sold supplies to Sengbe Pieh and his men, Lieutenant Gedney and the USS *Washington* crew, and finally, Ruiz and Montes. The third issue was what the exact nature of the cargo was. Were the African slaves property or human beings?

THE *AMISTAD* TRIAL SPARKED DEBATE ABOUT SLAVERY IN THE UNITED STATES.
WHILE ABOLITIONISTS OPPOSED THE PRACTICE OF OWNING HUMAN BEINGS,
PLANTATION OWNERS WERE AFRAID OF LOSING SLAVE LABOR.

Many other issues arose before the *Amistad* trial started. The case caused national and international conflict. Within the United States, some people favored slavery and others opposed it. In the South, wealthy plantation owners who depended on slave labor wanted the *Amistad* Africans to be considered property. On the other side, abolitionists wanted the *Amistad* Africans set free. They believed that the Africans had a right to fight against being enslaved.

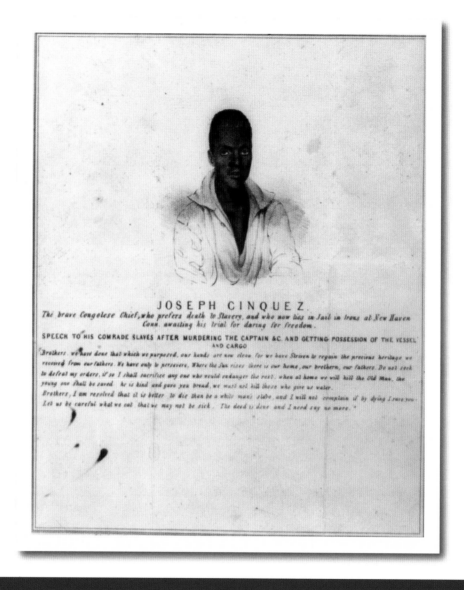

JOSEPH CINQUEZ.

The brave Congolese Chief, who prefers death to Slavery, and who now lies in Jail in Irons at New Haven Conn. awaiting his trial for daring for freedom.

SPEECH TO HIS COMRADE SLAVES AFTER MURDERING THE CAPTAIN &C. AND GETTING POSSESSION OF THE VESSEL AND CARGO

"Brothers, we have done that which we purposed, our hands are now clean for we have Striven to regain the precious heritage we received from our fathers. We have only to persevere. Where the Sun rises there is our home, our brethren, our fathers. Do not seek to defeat my orders, if so I shall sacrifice any one who would endanger the rest, when at home we will kill the Old Man, the young one shall be saved. he is kind and gave you bread, we must not kill those who give us water.

Brothers, I am resolved that it is better to die than be a white mans slave, and I will not complain if by dying I save you. Let us be careful what we eat that we may not be sick. The deed is done and I need say no more."

Outside of the United States, the government of Spain objected because the *Amistad* and its cargo had belonged to Spanish citizens. They wanted the ship and all its cargo—including the Africans—returned to Ruiz and Montes. The Spanish government pressured President Martin Van Buren to return the *Amistad.* It seemed, however, that the decision rested with the courts, not the president.

Van Buren expected trouble with politicians from the South and with the Spanish if the court ruled in favor of the slaves. So, Van Buren ordered the skipper of a schooner docked in New Haven harbor, the USS *Grampus,* to take the Mendians to Cuba if that should be the decision of the court. All this happened before the trial had even started!

PRESIDENT MARTIN VAN BUREN WANTED TO RETURN THE *AMISTAD* AFRICANS TO CUBA.

The Trial

A number of famous—and not so famous—people were involved in the *Amistad* trial. It was not a jury trial. That meant a judge would decide the **verdict.** Again, the judge was Andrew T. Judson. **Attorney** William S. Holabird presented the government's case against the *Amistad* Africans. The lawyers defending the Africans included Roger S. Baldwin, Seth Staples, and Theodore Sedgwick. These men were famous lawyers in the 1830s.

ANDREW T. JUDSON SERVED AS THE JUDGE IN THE FIRST *AMISTAD* TRIAL.

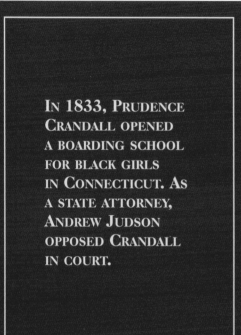

IN 1833, PRUDENCE
CRANDALL OPENED
A BOARDING SCHOOL
FOR BLACK GIRLS
IN CONNECTICUT. AS
A STATE ATTORNEY,
ANDREW JUDSON
OPPOSED CRANDALL
IN COURT.

Andrew Judson had earned a name for himself as someone who favored slavery. In 1833, as a state attorney in Connecticut, Judson had tried Prudence Crandall for running a school that taught African-American girls in Canterbury, Connecticut. She was found guilty, but the decision was later reversed. An angry mob set fire to her school, however, and Crandall left the state. Judson had been a judge for four years when the *Amistad* trial came to his courtroom.

William Holabird did not want the *Amistad* case to go to trial. He hoped President Van Buren would solve the problem for him by swift presidential action. However, Holabird clearly favored slavery.

In a letter to a fellow lawyer, he said, "I should regret extremely if the rascally blacks should fall into the hands of the abolitionists, with whom Hartford [Connecticut] is filled."

ABOLITIONISTS RALLIED AROUND THE CAUSE OF FREEDOM DURING THE *AMISTAD* TRIAL. IN THIS ENGRAVING, BLACKS AND WHITES GATHER FOR AN ANTISLAVERY MEETING IN BOSTON, MASSACHUSETTS.

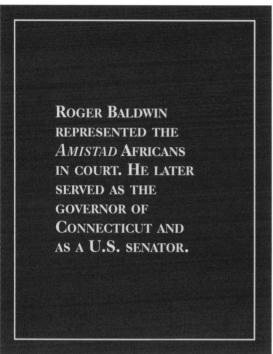

ROGER BALDWIN REPRESENTED THE *AMISTAD* AFRICANS IN COURT. HE LATER SERVED AS THE GOVERNOR OF CONNECTICUT AND AS A U.S. SENATOR.

Abolitionists chose Roger Baldwin to lead the defense team. In 1831, Baldwin opposed an angry mob protesting the building of a training school for African-Americans. His plan to defend the *Amistad* Africans included accusing Ruiz and Montes of being criminals. He hoped to prove that the Mendians should not be considered property because they were never truly slaves.

The trial began in September 1839. Sengbe Pieh and the other Mendians arrived in the courtroom. The defense lawyer called Sengbe Pieh to the witness stand. James Covey translated the Africans' story for the court.

Covey explained that the Mendians had been among 500 or more Africans taken to Cuba on the Portuguese ship *Tecora*. After being placed in a barracoon, they were sold to Ruiz and Montes. Then, they had boarded the *Amistad*. The Africans told of the trip to Guanaja. They told about the cook's threat to kill and eat them and described their fight against their owners. The court heard about how the slaves were chained and beaten, starved and denied water, then jailed.

The court also heard from Ruiz and Montes. They claimed that the Africans were ladinos and, therefore, legally slaves. Ruiz and Montes presented their false papers.

Baldwin argued against the claim that the Africans were ladinos. He said, "Here are three children, between the ages of seven and nine years, who are proved to be native Africans. . . . They were not born slaves, they were born in Africa." Baldwin pointed out that none of the Africans spoke Spanish, the language of Cuba. Finally, he argued that the Africans were not property but people.

It took several months to reach a decision in the Amistad case. The Africans remained in jail the entire time.

WITH THE HELP OF A MENDI TRANSLATOR, THE AFRICANS WERE ABLE TO DESCRIBE THEIR WRETCHED CONDITIONS ABOARD THE *AMISTAD* TO THE COURT. IN THIS ENGRAVING SHOWING SIMILAR CONDITIONS, SLAVES ARE SHACKLED BEFORE BEING PUT IN THE SHIP'S HOLD IN THE 1830s.

On January 15, 1840, Judge Judson delivered his verdict. He said that Lieutenant Gedney and his crew could claim salvage of the *Amistad* and its cargo. But, he added, the Africans were not part of that cargo. Judson ruled that the cabin boy and slave Antonio should be returned to his owners in Cuba.

THE *AMISTAD* TRIAL TOOK PLACE IN THE SENATE CHAMBER AT THE OLD STATE HOUSE IN HARTFORD, CONNECTICUT. THE BUILDING WAS CONSTRUCTED IN 1789.

The most surprising thing Judson said was that the Africans were neither slaves nor Spanish subjects. They were free men and women. Judson added, "Cinque [Sengbe Pieh] and Grabeau shall not sigh for Africa in vain." Judson recommended that President Van Buren have a ship take the Africans home.

Although the abolitionists had won, they were still concerned that Van Buren would send the Africans back to Cuba to please the Spanish. To protect the Africans, the abolitionists took the case to the U.S. Supreme Court. Baldwin continued as the Africans' lawyer. The abolitionists also asked John Quincy Adams, former president of the United States, to speak for the Africans.

JOHN QUINCY ADAMS, WHO SERVED AS PRESIDENT OF THE UNITED STATES FROM 1825 TO 1829, AGREED TO DEFEND THE *AMISTAD* AFRICANS IN THE U.S. SUPREME COURT.

In the Supreme Court case, government lawyers argued that the papers for the *Amistad* were correct. Because the papers were in order, the Africans were slaves and property of Ruiz and Montes. These lawyers said that Spain demanded that the Africans be returned to Cuba, where they would be tried again for mutiny and murder.

Baldwin rose for the defense. He said that a U.S. court had already declared the Africans free people. As free people, he said, they had the right to fight against being enslaved.

Then John Quincy Adams spoke. He said that President Van Buren had no interest in justice. Adams said that right and wrong did not matter to Van Buren as long as the Spanish were happy with the result. Adams pointed out that the president had no say in matters of the courts, according to the laws set up in the U.S. Constitution.

Finally, the Supreme Court ruled. The judges said that the Africans had never been legally the property or slaves of Ruiz and Montes. They were not pirates, robbers, or murderers. They were free people who had been kidnapped from their homes.

The court turned the Africans over to a group called the *Amistad* Committee. The group worked to raise money to transport the Africans back to their homeland. Since the beginning of their dark journey, 18 of the Africans from the *Amistad* had died. It took many more months before the *Amistad* Committee could collect enough money to pay for the trip.

JUSTICE JOSEPH STORY WROTE AND READ THE U.S. SUPREME COURT'S 1841 DECISION IN THE *AMISTAD* CASE. THE COURT RULED THAT THE *AMISTAD* AFRICANS WERE FREE INDIVIDUALS WHO HAD BEEN TAKEN AGAINST THEIR WILL AND TRANSPORTED ILLEGALLY.

1.

Supreme Court of the United States.
January Term 1841.

The United States. App.ts
42.   vs
The Libellants & Claimants of the
Schooner Amistad, her tackle
apparel and furniture, together
with her Cargo, and the Africans
mentioned and described in
the several Libels and Claims.

On Appeal from the Cir-
cuit Court of the United
States for the District
of Connecticut.

Mr. Justice Story delivered
the opinion of the Court.

This is the case of an appeal
from the decree of the Circuit Court of the District of
Connecticut sitting in Admiralty. The leading facts
as they appear upon the Transcript of the proceedings
are as follows.

On the 27th of June, 1839, the Schooner L.
Amistad, being the property of Spanish Subjects,
cleared out from the port of Havanna, in the Island
of Cuba, for Puerto Principe in the same Island. On
board of the Schooner were the Captain Ransom Ferrer,
and Jose Ruiz and Pedro Montez, all Spanish Subjects. The former had with him a Negro boy named
Antonio, claimed to be his slave. Jose Ruiz had with
him forty nine Negroes, claimed by him as his slaves,
and stated to be his property in a certain pass or docu-
ment signed by the Governor General of Cuba. Pedro

A Legacy of Freedom

The *Amistad* trial increased awareness of the slavery issue in the United States. The abolitionists considered the verdicts in both courts to be victories against slavery. Those in favor of slavery said the verdicts did not affect slaves in the United States. Both sides were right.

The *Amistad* Africans were declared free people and not possessions. However, slaves within the United States were still considered property of their owners. In this regard, nothing had changed.

Spain continued to press the U.S. government about the *Amistad* verdicts. They wanted payment for the loss of the ship and its cargo, including the Africans. They never received a penny. They wanted the *Amistad* Africans returned to Cuba, which did not happen.

Antonio, the cabin boy who had been declared a slave, was supposed to be sent back to Cuba. Mysteriously, he disappeared. A year or so after the trial ended, Antonio reappeared in Canada. Abolitionists had helped him flee the United States to live in Montreal, Quebec.

Many people were outraged that President Van Buren had tried to force the courts to rule against the *Amistad* Africans. The *Hartford Courant* newspaper attacked Van Buren and his handling of the *Amistad* case. It wrote, "Surely Martin Van Buren is playing the part of a tyrant with a high hand—else why this tampering with our courts of justice." People turned against Van Buren for trying to influence the courts. He was defeated in the next presidential election by William Henry Harrison.

THE U.S. SUPREME COURT DECLARED THE *AMISTAD* AFRICANS FREE IN 1841, BUT
SLAVERY WAS NOT ABOLISHED IN THE COUNTRY UNTIL 1865. HERE AFRICAN-AMERICANS
IN WASHINGTON, D.C., CELEBRATE FREEDOM IN 1866.

As for the *Amistad* Africans, they finally made it back to Sierra Leone. On November 27, 1841, the remaining 35 Mendians and a group of **missionaries** boarded the *Gentleman* for the trip home. The journey took seven weeks. When they landed in Sierra Leone, Kin-na, one of the Mendians who had learned English, wrote to Lewis Tappan. He said, "We have reached Sierra Leone and one little while after we go to Mendi and we land very safely."

The missionaries who traveled with the *Amistad* Africans founded a Christian mission in Sierra Leone in 1842. Many of the Mendians stayed at the mission. Sengbe Pieh, however, chose to go home to his family. When he arrived, he found that his wife and children had died. He did not return to the mission until 1879. Old and sickly, Sengbe Pieh had returned to die.

AFTER WINNING HIS TRIAL IN THE UNITED STATES, MENDI LEADER SENGBE PIEH RETURNED TO HIS HOMELAND OF SIERRA LEONE. THIS HELMET MASK IS A WORK OF ART MADE BY THE MENDI PEOPLE.

Timeline

Early 1500s	European nations begin shipping African captives to the Americas to work as slaves.
1799	New York passes a law saying that all children born to enslaved persons after July 4, 1799, are to be freed at age 28 for men and age 25 for women.
Early 1800s	Abolitionists speak out against slavery in the United States.
1817	Spain signs a treaty with Great Britain, ending foreign slave trade in all Spanish lands.
1820	Legal slave trade ends in Cuba. Illegal slave trade continues.
1837– 1839	Slave traders bring 25,000 Africans to Cuba. Many Africans die on the trip.
1839	In spring, Sengbe Pieh is captured from Sierra Leone. He ends up on the Portuguese ship *Tecora* with more than 500 other Africans bound for Havana, Cuba, to be sold into slavery. In Havana, he and 52 other Africans are purchased and, in June, loaded on the *Amistad* to sail to Guanaja, Cuba. On July 1, Sengbe Pieh helps lead a mutiny. In August, the *Amistad* is taken to New London, Connecticut, where the Africans are charged with mutiny and murder. In September, the *Amistad* trial begins.
1840	Judge Andrew T. Judson rules that the Africans are to be turned over to U.S. president Martin Van Buren and returned to Africa.
1841	In February, the U.S. Supreme Court hears the case and rules that the Africans are free people who were kidnapped from their homes. In November, the *Gentleman* sails to Sierra Leone with 35 surviving Mendians and a group of missionaries.
1842	The Christian missionaries who traveled with the *Amistad* Africans found the Mendi Mission in Sierra Leone.
1879	An old man, Sengbe Pieh returns to the mission to die.

Glossary

abolitionists (AB-uh-LISH-uhn-ists)
Abolitionists were people who worked against slavery in the 1800s in the United States. Abolitionists did not believe in the practice of owning human beings.

attorney (uh-TUR-nee)
An attorney is a lawyer. In the *Amistad* trial, the attorney who presented the government's case against the Africans was William Holabird.

barracoons (bar-uh-KOONZ)
Barracoons are large, plain buildings used as prisons. Slaves in Cuba lived in barracoons until they were sold at the slave market.

holds (HOHLDZ)
Holds are the parts of ships where cargo is stored. Slave traders packed as many Africans in their ships' holds as possible.

indigo (IN-duh-goh)
Indigo is a plant with berries that can be used to make a purple-blue dye. Plantations in the South grew cotton, tobacco, sugar, coffee, and indigo.

manacles (MAA-nuh-kles)
Manacles are a type of handcuffs. The *Amistad* slaves wore manacles that cut their wrists.

missionaries (MISH-uh-ner-eez)
Missionaries are people who travel to foreign lands to teach their faith and do other charitable works. The Mendians returned to Sierra Leone with a group of missionaries who hoped to bring Christianity to the people there.

mutiny (MYU-tuh-nee)
A mutiny is an open rebellion against the people in charge, often on a ship. The *Amistad* captives Sengbe Pieh, Grabeau, and Burnah led a mutiny against the ship's captain and crew.

salvage (SAL-vij)
Salvage is payment for finding a lost ship, cargo, or both. Gedney and his men hoped to claim the *Amistad*, its cargo, and the slaves as salvage.

schooner (SKOO-nur)
A schooner is a fast-sailing ship with two masts. In 1839, Pedro Montes, José Ruiz, their crew, and their 53 Mendi slaves left for the Americas on a schooner called the *Amistad*.

shackles (SHA-kles)
Shackles are chains on the legs or arms of a prisoner. The slave traders put iron shackles around Sengbe Pieh's ankles.

verdict (VUHR-dikt)
The verdict is the decision of the judge or jury in a trial. In the *Amistad* trial, Judge Andrew Judson delivered the verdict.

Index

Further Information

Books

Freedman, Suzanne. *United States v. Amistad: Rebellion on a Slave Ship.* Berkeley Heights, N.J.: Enslow Publishers, 2000.

Jurmain, Suzanne. *Freedom's Sons: The True Story of the Amistad Mutiny.* New York: Lothrop, Lee & Shepard Books, 1998.

Myers, Walter Dean. *Amistad: A Long Road to Freedom.* New York: Dutton Children's Books, 1998.

Sterne, Emma Gelders. *The Story of the Amistad.* Mineola, N.Y.: Dover Publications, 2001.

Web Sites

Visit our homepage for lots of links about the *Amistad* Mutiny:

http://www.childsworld.com/links.html

Note to Parents, Teachers, and Librarians:
We routinely verify our Web links to make sure they're safe,
active sites—so encourage your readers to check them out!

About the Author

Barbara A. Somervill is the author of dozens of nonfiction books for young readers. She also writes video scripts and textbooks. She enjoys reading, painting, doing needlework, and playing bridge. She is a graduate of Saint Lawrence University in Canton, New York.